CONTENTS

WILD, WET AND WINDY

Claire Llewellyn

CANDLEWICK PRESS
CAMBRIDGE, MASSACHUSETTS

1 Scientists who study the weather are called meteorologists. At weather centers they look at photographs taken by satellites high above Earth. Large spiraling clouds show where a hurricane is starting to form over the ocean.

2 The meteorologists figure out when and where the hurricane is likely to hit the coast. About 36 hours before it strikes, they send out weather warnings on TV and radio.

3 People who live in the danger area decide whether to stay or go. Either way, they try to make their homes safe by boarding up the windows and doors.

4 Sitting through a hurricane is terrifying. The wind roars around the house, tearing at the roof, screaming at the doors and windows, and hurling garbage cans, branches, and anything else it can pick up against the walls.

5 It can take as long as 18 hours for a hurricane to pass by completely. As soon as it's all over, everyone goes outside to check the damage. Then it's time to start cleaning up the mess!

1 The wind is rising. A sudden gust screams in from the sea, then dies down, leaving an eerie calm — the lull before the storm.

2 With every hour the sky gets darker and the wind grows stronger. Rain starts falling — heavy stinging drops driven sideways by the wind.

STORMY WEATHER

3 The palm trees bend wildly, their spiky leaves blasted by the wind. This is no ordinary storm — there's a hurricane on the way!

4 Hurricanes are among the most dangerous storms on Earth. They can flatten forests, smash houses, and overturn cars. They can even tear the clothes off your back.

5 They bring towering waves surging up the shore, wrecking boats and beach huts, flooding shops, cafés, and people's precious homes.

6 Hurricanes start over warm tropical seas to the north and south of the equator. Hot steamy air rises quickly from the water, forming thick clouds that start to spin.

4 HURRICANES

7 Day by day the storm grows bigger and more powerful. Within a week, it's hundreds of miles wide — a mass of swirling winds, moving slowly but surely toward land.

8 The hurricane hits the coast with devastating force. But on dry land there's no damp sea air to feed it, and hour by hour it slowly blows itself out.

9 In some parts of the world, hurricanes are called cyclones, typhoons, or Willy-Willies. But they're all the same sort of storm — and they all spell trouble!

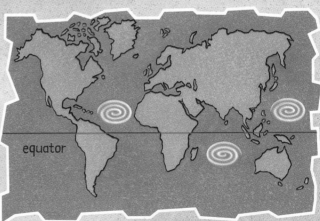

equator

HURRICANES 5

BREEZING ALONG

1 People have been putting the wind to work for thousands of years — if only to get their wash dry!

2 About 5,500 years ago, the ancient Egyptians were the first people to put sails on their ships.

3 In China about 3,000 years later, the very first kites were being flown. Some were even used to lift people above battles so they could spy on the enemy!

2 It's the sun that makes air move. Sunshine warms the land and sea, and they in turn heat the air above them.

3 Hot air is light, so it floats up into the sky. This doesn't leave a gap lower down, though, because more air flows in to take its place.

4 And it's all this air flowing and moving about that makes the wind.

5 The world's winds move the weather along, bringing warm or chilly days, clear skies or rain. That's why a change in the wind often brings a change in the weather.

4 Windmills were first built about 1,350 years ago in Persia (now Iran). Their sails turned millstones, which ground grain into flour.

5 The world's first wind farm was built in the 1970s in Washington. As the blades on the wind machines turn, they drive machinery that produces electricity.

WIND 7

WHIRLING WINDS

1 Long and gray like an elephant's trunk, a tornado screams past at more than 35 miles per hour.

2 It's a giant vacuum cleaner, pulling up trees, barns, tractors, animals — everything in its path. It doesn't just snatch chickens, it even plucks them clean!

3 Tornadoes are whirling winds that form when a column of cold air sinks down from a thundercloud while lighter warm air rises up around it.

4 The warm air rises so quickly that it starts to spin, sucking up dirt from the ground and forming a dark whirling funnel that twists its way back to the cloud.

8 TORNADOES

5 Many tornadoes are only 300 or so feet wide across the base and last for less than an hour. They're much smaller than hurricanes and over much more quickly.

6 But don't be fooled. The winds in a tornado whiz around at more than 350 miles per hour. They're twice as fast as hurricane winds — and twice as powerful, too!

1 Some tornadoes start over lakes and seas. These whirling winds are called waterspouts, and they suck up soaking wet funnels of spray.

2 In the past, they were mistaken for long-necked sea monsters. Some people think a waterspout lies behind the legend of Scotland's Loch Ness Monster.

3 Waterspouts spin more gently than tornadoes, but they're still strong enough to pick a boat clean up out of the water.

4 They've been known to suck up animals, too. Frogs, toads, and ducks have all been plucked out of ponds or lakes and dropped down in a shower of "rain." So if your umbrella is suddenly pelted by fish, you'll know that a waterspout was to blame!

DRIPPING WET

1 Drip, patter, plop! It's raining again. Fat wet raindrops bounce off the leaves and stream down onto the ground.

2 Nearly every living thing depends on rain. Without it, no plants would grow, and there would be nothing for animals to eat or drink.

3 Rain never falls from a clear blue sky — only from clouds. Clouds are made up of billions of water droplets and ice crystals, which are so tiny they float in the air.

10 RAIN

4 But the droplets and crystals don't stay tiny. They bump into one another, growing bigger and heavier all the time.

5 Then, when they're too heavy to float, they fall to the ground as rain or snow.

6 By now, some of the raindrops are the size of small peas — that's a million times bigger than when they floated in the cloud.

1 The world's water moves on a never-ending journey from the sky to the land and sea and back again. This is the water cycle.

2 Showers of rain feed rivers, lakes, and seas, and leave puddles on the ground. The sun's heat turns the water into an invisible gas called water vapor, which mixes with the air and rises into the sky. The change from a liquid to a gas is called evaporation.

3 The higher you go above the ground, the colder it gets. So as air rises, it cools. Eventually, it gets so cold that the vapor turns back into tiny water droplets. This change from a gas to a liquid is called condensation.

4 The tiny droplets form clouds, then slowly grow into raindrops. At last, they fall back to Earth — and the whole cycle starts all over again!

1 Lighthouses were probably invented by the ancient Egyptians. For more than 5,000 years, these bright lights have guided sailors past rocks and sandbars on foggy days and moonless nights.

2 But as recently as 200 years ago, there were people called wreckers who set dreadful traps for ships, to get their hands on the valuable cargo.

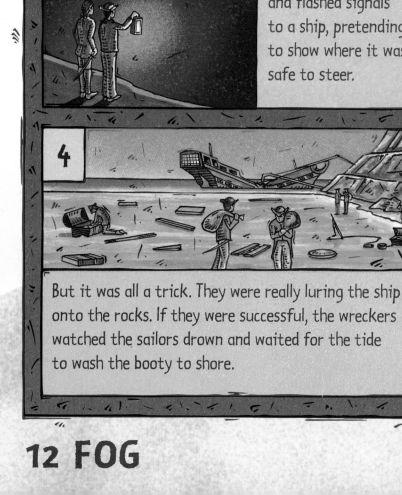

3 These wreckers stood on a rocky promontory and flashed signals to a ship, pretending to show where it was safe to steer.

4 But it was all a trick. They were really luring the ship onto the rocks. If they were successful, the wreckers watched the sailors drown and waited for the tide to wash the booty to shore.

1 The beam from a lighthouse cuts through the fog. Out on the water, anxious sailors keep their distance, or their ship might end up on the rocks!

2 You can't see far in fog — that's why it's so dangerous at sea. It's dangerous on land, too, so many cars have fog lights — their own mini-lighthouse beams!

MISTY AND MURKY

3 Fog is chilly and damp, and walking through it is like walking inside a cloud.

4 That's because fog is made up of billions of floating water droplets — just like clouds.

5 And although it's much nearer to the ground, fog forms in the same way as clouds — warm air cools and the vapor in it turns back into droplets of water.

YOU CAN ONLY SEE UP TO 15 FEET IN FOG—TRUE OR FALSE?

FOG 13

SUMMER SOAKING

1 It's June in India and the streets are awash. The rainy season, the monsoon, has arrived at last.

2 India's monsoon season lasts from June to September, and these four months bring nearly the whole year's rain. There's precious little at any other time of year.

3 Some parts of the world have four seasons — spring, summer, fall, and winter. India has two main seasons — wet and dry.

1 Most of the world's rice is grown — and eaten — in India, southern China, and other places with wet and dry seasons. Rice seeds are sown toward the end of the dry season, when the rains are just weeks away.

2 The seedlings grow best in lots of water, so they're moved to paddy fields. These have low mud walls, which trap the monsoon rains.

4 India isn't unusual, though. Other countries in the tropics, the warmest parts of the world, also have wet and dry seasons.

5 Wet seasons can cause problems. In the worst years, the monsoon rains turn trickling streams into roaring rivers, and raging floods snatch homes, livestock, and lives.

6 But the rain isn't all bad. Without each summer's deluge, the rice crop would fail. And without rice, many people would starve.

3 By the end of the wet season the plants are high and green, and their heads are heavy with rice grains.

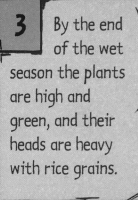

4 The return of the dry season brings hot sunny days. The ground dries out and the crop ripens. Soon the rice is golden and ready for harvesting.

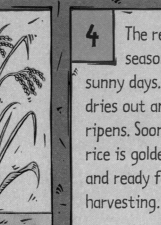

MONSOONS 15

1 It was an American scientist named Benjamin Franklin who showed that lightning is a kind of electricity. He did this back in 1752 by carrying out a dangerous experiment.

2 Franklin knew that electricity would flow through some materials, such as water and some kinds of metal. So he flew a kite in a thunderstorm with a metal door key dangling from the string.

3 Sure enough, small electrical sparks jumped down from a thundercloud and ran along the wet string to the key. Franklin was lucky, though. A big bolt of lightning would have killed him!

4 Franklin put his experiment to good use by inventing the lightning conductor — a metal rod fixed to the roof of tall buildings with a thick metal strap running from it into the ground. If lightning strikes the rod, it doesn't damage the building. It just flows down the strap and safely into the ground.

1 Some people say that lightning never strikes twice in the same place. Well, they're wrong. The Eiffel Tower in Paris is struck about 25 times every year!

2 A flash of lightning is a long finger of electricity that slices through the sky at up to 90,000 miles a second.

3 Each flash carries so much power that it could keep a light bulb burning for more than 300 years.

FLASH, BANG, CRASH

5 As the droplets and crystals whirl up and down, the cloud starts to crackle with electricity.

6 Suddenly, a giant spark surges to the ground and shoots back up to the cloud with a blinding flash.

4 Lightning begins inside towering thunderclouds, where strong winds pick up the water droplets and ice crystals and hurl them around.

7 Lightning is about five times hotter than the surface of the sun. Its burning path heats the air so quickly that it booms — with an earsplitting crack of thunder!

LIGHTNING 17

DRY AS DUST

1 Struggling through a sandstorm is a nightmare — even for people who live in the Sahara Desert in North Africa.

2 Howling winds whip up clouds of sand and dust that fly everywhere — cutting faces and hands, blowing into eyes, ears, noses, and mouths.

3 Deserts are windy places, but they're not all sandy. Some are covered with gravel and pebbles. Others are simply bare rock.

18 DESERTS

4 To scientists, a desert is a place with ten inches or less of rain a year.

5 But the rain doesn't fall evenly every year. One year, there may be no rain. The next, it may all come in one tremendous storm.

6 Although it can change from day to day, desert weather is usually dry and sunny. The pattern of weather in a particular place is called its climate.

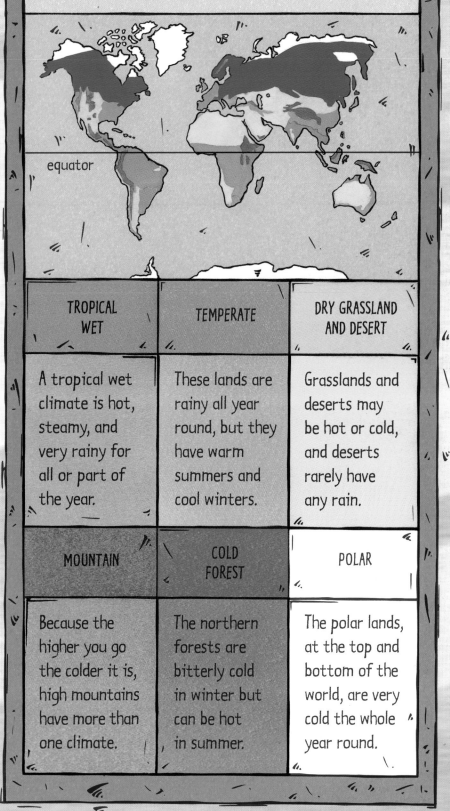

Every region in the world has its own climate, and different climates largely depend on how close a place is to the equator. It is hottest near the equator and coldest at the North and South Poles.

equator

TROPICAL WET	TEMPERATE	DRY GRASSLAND AND DESERT
A tropical wet climate is hot, steamy, and very rainy for all or part of the year.	These lands are rainy all year round, but they have warm summers and cool winters.	Grasslands and deserts may be hot or cold, and deserts rarely have any rain.
MOUNTAIN	**COLD FOREST**	**POLAR**
Because the higher you go the colder it is, high mountains have more than one climate.	The northern forests are bitterly cold in winter but can be hot in summer.	The polar lands, at the top and bottom of the world, are very cold the whole year round.

CLIMATE 19

1 Animals that live in snowy places have different ways of getting through the freezing temperatures and bitter winds of winter. Some of them hide away in caves or burrows, spending the cold dark months in a kind of deep sleep called hibernation.

2 Adult polar bears have such warm fur that they don't normally need to hibernate. But the females do if they're pregnant, as their newborn cubs don't have thick-enough fur. The cubs are born in midwinter in dens under the snow.

3 Not all animals hibernate, though. Hamsterlike creatures called lemmings are busy all winter long. They keep out of the icy winds by building runways under the snow, where they nibble on plants until spring returns.

4 The penguins that live in Antarctica have to stick out the worst winters on Earth. The birds huddle together in huge groups to keep one another warm. And the whole flock slowly shuffles around so that as few birds as possible are chilled by the howling wind.

5 But some animals could never survive the cold. So in the fall many creatures leave their summer homes and fly, walk, or swim to places where the winter weather is much kinder.

WHITEOUT!

2 This high up, the air is so cold in winter that snow doesn't melt, even in sunshine. With each fresh fall, it gets deeper and deeper.

1 A skier whizzes down a mountain on hissing skis. The snow looks beautiful and feels firm enough — but is it safe?

3 But in spring, as the weather gets warmer, the snow starts to melt and may suddenly slip. Within seconds, it's surging downhill at breakneck speed...

4 this is an avalanche — and it can be deadly!

5 The worst avalanches are nearly 350 feet wide and roar down the mountainside at about 200 miles per hour — much too fast for people to escape.

6 The crashing snow sends up huge clouds of icy dust and buries everything in its path — homes, villages, train tracks, roads....

7 Many other things can set an avalanche moving — an earthquake, a thunderclap, or even a sudden gust of wind.

8 To make mountains safer, snow patrols keep an eye on the higher slopes. In some places, they even use explosives to trigger an avalanche when people are out of harm's way.

Snowflakes are tiny water droplets that have frozen into crystals of ice high up in clouds. Sometimes the crystals melt into raindrops as they fall. But if the air is very cold they stay frozen, and we have snow.

INDEX

Main illustrations by Robin Budden (10–11); Chris Forsey (cover, 3–5, 8–9);
Christian Hook (14–15, 18–19); Mike Lister (6–7, 16–17); Darren Pattenden (21–23);
Peter Visscher (12–13); inset and picture-strip illustrations by Ian Thompson
Thanks to Helicopter Graphix and the Wildlife Art Agency
Designed by Jonathan Hair and Matthew Lilly, and edited by Jackie Gaff
Consultants: Keith Lye and Steve Parker
Text copyright © 1997 by Claire Llewellyn
Illustrations copyright © 1997 by Walker Books Ltd.
All rights reserved.
First U.S. edition 1997
Library of Congress Cataloging-in-Publication Data is available.
Library of Congress Catalog Card Number 96-44371
ISBN 0-7636-0304-X
2 4 6 8 10 9 7 5 3 1
Printed in Italy
This book was typeset in Kosmik.
Candlewick Press
2067 Massachusetts Avenue
Cambridge, Massachusetts 02140

QUIZ ANSWERS

Page 2 — FALSE
Hurricane winds only blow clockwise south of the equator. North of the equator they blow the opposite way — counterclockwise.

Page 7 — FALSE
The only planets without winds are Mercury and Pluto. Neptune is the windiest planet, with windstorms that gust at around 1,300 mph!

Page 8 — TRUE
Tornadoes happen over all the world's big landmasses. In the United States, there are about 500 tornadoes every year.

Page 10 — FALSE
Raindrops are little flattened balls of water in the shape of hamburger buns.

Page 13 — FALSE
To a scientist, it's a foggy day even when you can see things that are up to 3,280 feet away. If you can see any farther, the weather is considered misty.

Page 15 — FALSE
The world's wettest place is Mount Waialeale in Hawaii. It rains there 350 days a year.

Page 17 — TRUE
We see lightning before we hear thunder because light travels faster than sound.

Page 18 — TRUE
The world's driest desert is the Atacama Desert in Chile, South America. Until 1971 it hadn't rained there for 400 years.

Page 20 — FALSE
Some snowflakes are star shaped, but others are long and needlelike.